WILD GUIDE NIGHT SKY
STAR FINDER

STORM DUNLOP; ILLUSTRATED BY WIL TIRION

HarperCollins*Publishers*

HarperCollins*Publishers*
77–85 Fulham Palace Road
London W6 8JB

The HarperCollins website address is:

www.**fire**and**water**.com

Collins is a registered trademark of HarperCollins*Publishers* Ltd.

10 9 8 7 6 5 4 3 2 1

05 04 03 02 01 00

ISBN 0 00 710083 3

Designed by Liz Bourne
Manufactured in China for Imago

USING THE STAR FINDER

The most commonly asked question in astronomy is 'What was that bright star I saw last night?' Anyone who has been asked this question knows that the answer is not always quite as simple as it might seem. The appearance of the sky changes continuously, so the stars that you can see in the early evening are different from those visible later at night. Frequently, the 'bright star' is actually a planet, and they follow erratic, although predictable paths across the sky, and so often cause confusion.

The *Wild Guide Night Sky Star Finder*, together with this booklet, will answer that burning question and many more. It may be used in conjunction with *Wild Guide Night Sky* itself or on its own, and its handy size means that it may be taken anywhere. It will show you what stars are visible, and the diagrams in this booklet will help you to identify the various planets, as well as giving details of the phases of the Moon.

The Star Finder itself is a device, known as a 'planisphere', that may be adjusted to show just those stars that are visible at any particular time. Planispheres are very ancient, and although the date of the earliest is unknown, it is thought that a large planisphere was housed inside the Tower of the Winds – which still stands in Athens – built at some time between 100 and 50 BC. What is more, that planisphere seems to have been rotated by a water-driven mechanism, so that it showed the appearance of the sky at any time of the day or night. The same type of map of the sky was used in the medieval instrument called the astrolabe, so when you use the Star Finder you are following in a long, long line of astronomers.

Contents

How the Star Finder Works.................... 4

The Northern Sky.............................. 7

The Position of the Moon and Planets...... 10

Planetary Positions 2000...................... 12

Planetary Positions 2001...................... 16

Planetary Positions 2002...................... 20

Planetary Positions 2003...................... 24

Planetary Positions 2004...................... 28

HOW THE STAR FINDER WORKS

At first glance the Star Finder may look complicated, but it is really quite simple to understand and use. Although we now know that the stars are at very different distances from us, they all seem to lie on a vast sphere, the celestial sphere, centred on the Earth. Similarly, all other objects in the sky, such as the Sun, Moon, planets and comets, all appear to lie on the same sphere. It is divided into the northern and southern hemispheres by the celestial equator, which is shown as a continuous black line.

As the Earth rotates from on its axis once every day, so the celestial sphere appears to rotate in the opposite direction (from east to west) once a day, carrying all celestial objects with it. As seen from any particular point on Earth, the whole sky seems to rotate about a single point. From the northern hemisphere, this point is the North Celestial Pole, extremely close to the star called Polaris, otherwise known as the Pole Star. Rotating Star Finder's overlay mimics the rotation of the Earth.

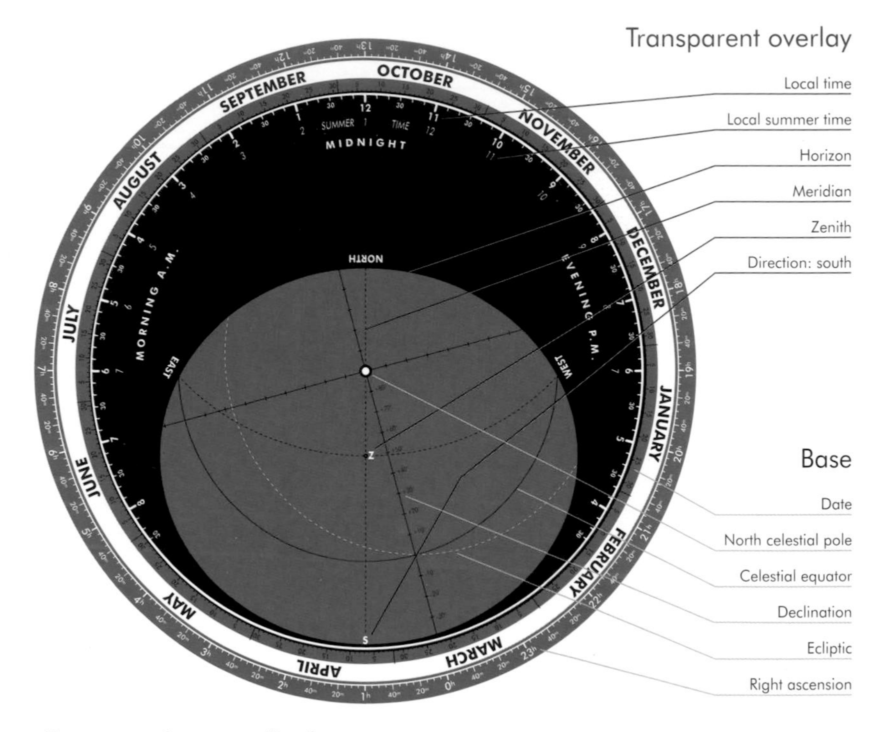

Stars and constellations

To make it easier to find their way around the night sky, since time immemorial people have given names both to individual bright stars, and also to particular groups of stars, or constellations. Many of the names and constellations are very old, some dating back to the Babylonians, and others to the Greek, Roman, and Arab astronomers. On the base chart, the constellation names are shown in capital letters (e.g., ANDROMEDA), and the names of bright stars as proper names with an initial capital letter (e.g., Capella). One cluster of stars, the Pleiades, is also shown in this way. Lines connect the stars in a particular constellation, to help you to identify them on the night sky. (Details of how to find and recognise all the northern constellations, together with a lot of other information, are given in the *Wild Guide Night Sky* book itself.)

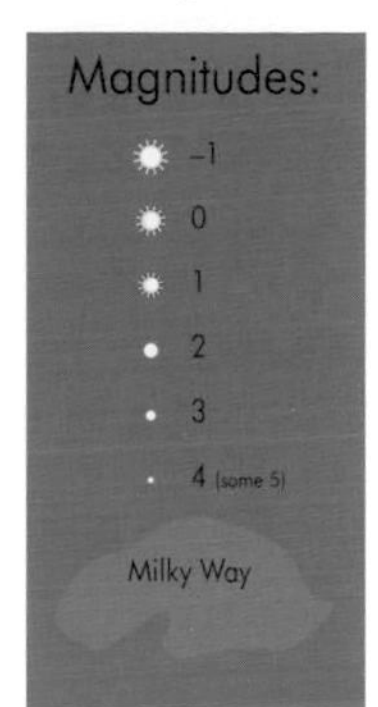

Stars are of different brightness (known as magnitude) and for historical reasons, the brightest were said to be of first magnitude, those slightly fainter, second magnitude, and so on. Star Finder shows all stars down to magnitude 4, with a few fainter ones to help with recognition of certain constellations. This limit is similar to that used for the monthly star charts in *Wild Guide Night Sky*.

What is visible tonight?

To find out what is visible in the sky tonight – or to identify that bright star someone has asked you about – simply set the time you want against the date. Make sure you use the markings for Mean Time (i.e., Winter Time) or Summer Time, as appropriate. The clear area of the overlay shows which stars and constellations are above the horizon. Don't forget, however, that for a few weeks around the time of the summer solstice, June 21, the sky never gets very dark, so you may be able to see the very brightest stars only. We will talk about identifying bright planets later.

If you hold Star Finder with the midnight mark (not the actual time) at the top, the lower portion shows you the sky looking south. The black dashed meridian line runs north-south, and crosses the curved east-west line at the zenith (marked 'Z'), directly overhead. To identify the stars in the north, turn Star Finder upside down. The constellations in this part of the sky, close to the North Pole, are visible every night. They are ideal guides when you start learning the sky. To help you to become familiar with them, especially as Polaris itself is hidden by Star Finder's pivot, they are shown in more detail on pp.7 8.

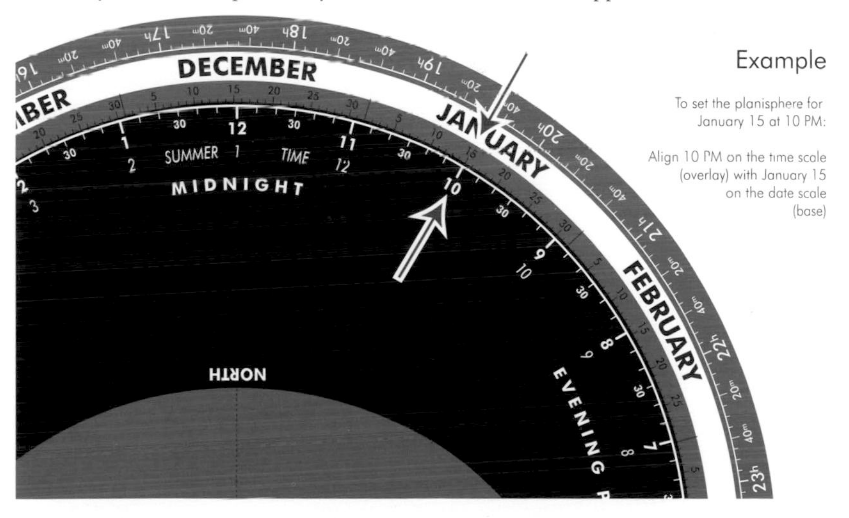

Example

To set the planisphere for January 15 at 10 PM:

Align 10 PM on the time scale (overlay) with January 15 on the date scale (base)

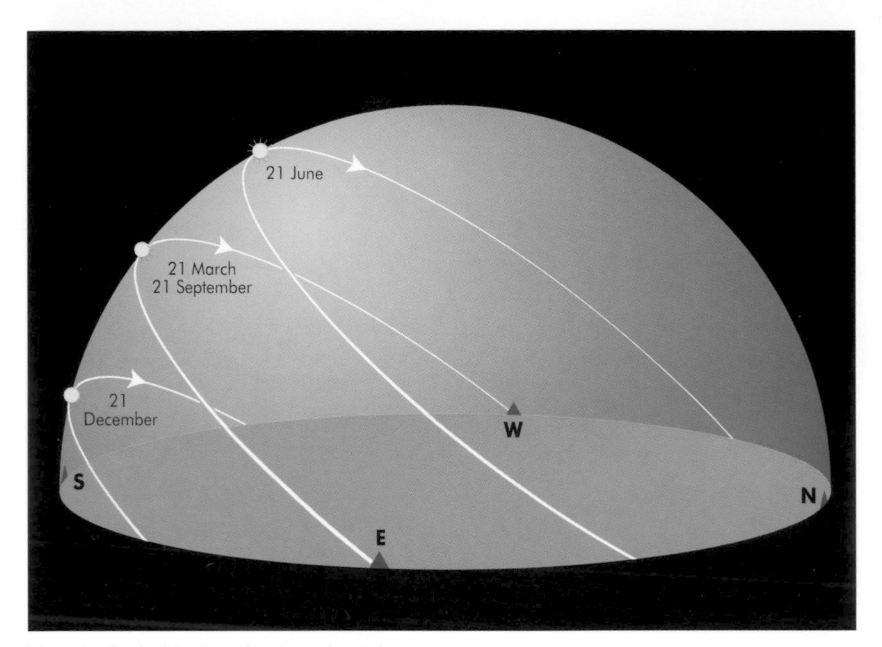

How the Sun's altitude varies throughout the year

The ecliptic and the Sun

Apart from its apparent daily motion from east to west, the Sun moves slowly from west to east across the sky during the course of the year. Its path is known as the ecliptic, and this is shown on the Star Finder by the dashed yellow line. The constellations through which the ecliptic runs are collectively known as the Zodiac, and this region of the sky is shown in the charts on p.11. Apart from the 12 well-known constellations, the ecliptic runs through the large constellation of Ophiuchus, and grazes the top of both Orion and Cetus.

You can find the approximate position of the Sun in the sky by using the meridian line on the overlay. Rotate the overlay so that the time of noon, 12:00 (the south point 'S') is set against the date. The Sun lies approximately where the meridian crosses the ecliptic. It is only approximate, because the Sun – and thus the time as shown by a sundial – is sometimes fast and sometimes slow when compared to our perfectly regular time-keeping. This is mainly because the Earth's orbit around the Sun is not a perfect circle, but an ellipse. The result is that the Earth does not move around the Sun at a constant speed, so it sometimes has to rotate a little more, and sometimes a little less than the average to bring the Sun back to the meridian. This difference is called the equation of time and may amount to as much as a quarter of an hour.

As everyone knows, the Sun's altitude above the horizon varies from winter to summer. This is because the Earth's rotational axis is not at right-angles to its orbit, but inclined at an angle. The northern and southern hemispheres are alternately tipped away from and towards the Sun, during their winter and summer, respectively. The black graduated lines on the base cross the ecliptic at the summer and winter solstices, when the sun is highest or lowest in the sky, and at the spring and autumnal equinoxes, when day and night are of equal length.

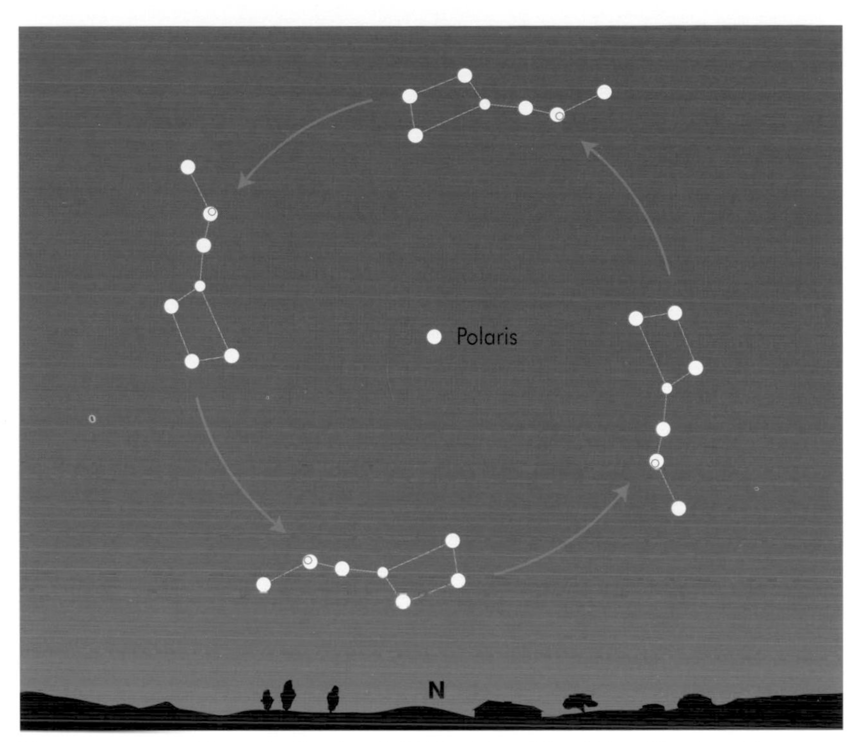

The approximate position of the Plough at 22:00 Mean Time (10 pm Winter Time, 9 pm Summer Time) for winter (right), spring, summer and autumn

The length of the day between sunrise and sunset varies greatly throughout the year. You can find the approximate times of sunrise and sunset from the Star Finder. First, find the position of the Sun. Holding the base still, rotate the overlay anticlockwise, until the horizon line touches that point in the sky. This is sunrise, and you can read off the approximate time against the date. Rotate the overlay clockwise to find the time of sunset. Again, the times are approximate because of the equation of time and other effects.

THE NORTHERN SKY

A few constellations that lie close to the North Celestial Pole (and therefore called circumpolar) are visible at any time of night, and throughout the year. They are always above the northern horizon, so are the best place to start learning the constellations. Nearly everyone can recognize the seven bright stars, known as the Plough (or Big Dipper in North America), which actually form part of the constellation of Ursa Major (the Great Bear). Although the Star Finder will show you exactly where they are, the diagram given here indicates their approximate position in the sky at different times of the year, and will help to ensure that you do not become confused.

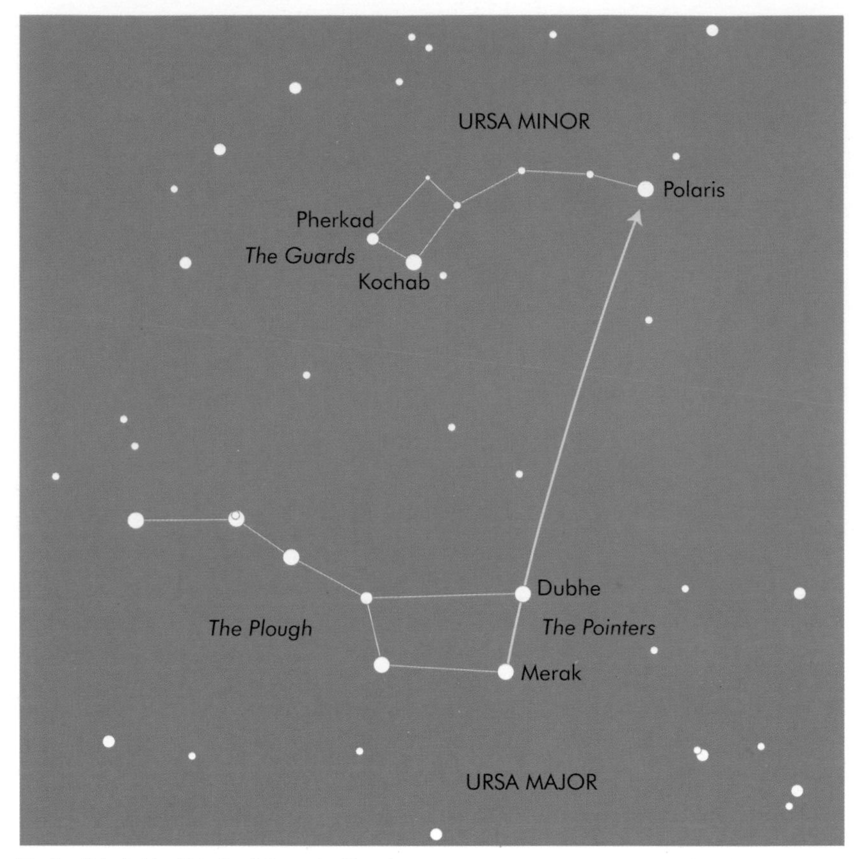

Finding Polaris (the Pole Star) from the Plough

Once you have found the Plough, follow the line of the two stars farthest from the 'tail' to Polaris, the Pole Star, around which all the other stars appear to circle, and which is hidden by Star Finder's pivot. This marks the end of the 'tail' of Ursa Minor (the Little Bear). Once you have found these markers, it will be easy to recognize some of the other constellations, such as the 'W' (or 'M') of Cassiopeia, more or less on the opposite side of the pole from Ursa Major and the bright stars Capella, in Auriga, or Deneb, in Cygnus. Capella is high overhead during the winter, and Deneb (together with Vega in Lyra) in summer.

The positions of the stars

The position of any object on the celestial sphere is given in a system of co-ordinates very similar to latitude and longitude on the Earth. These co-ordinates are known as declination and right ascension. Just as latitude is measured north or south of the Earth's equator, so declination is measured in degrees north (+) or south (-) of the celestial equator. It is shown on the base of the Star Finder by the black graduated lines. For clarity, figures are given only on the line that passes through the spring equinox.

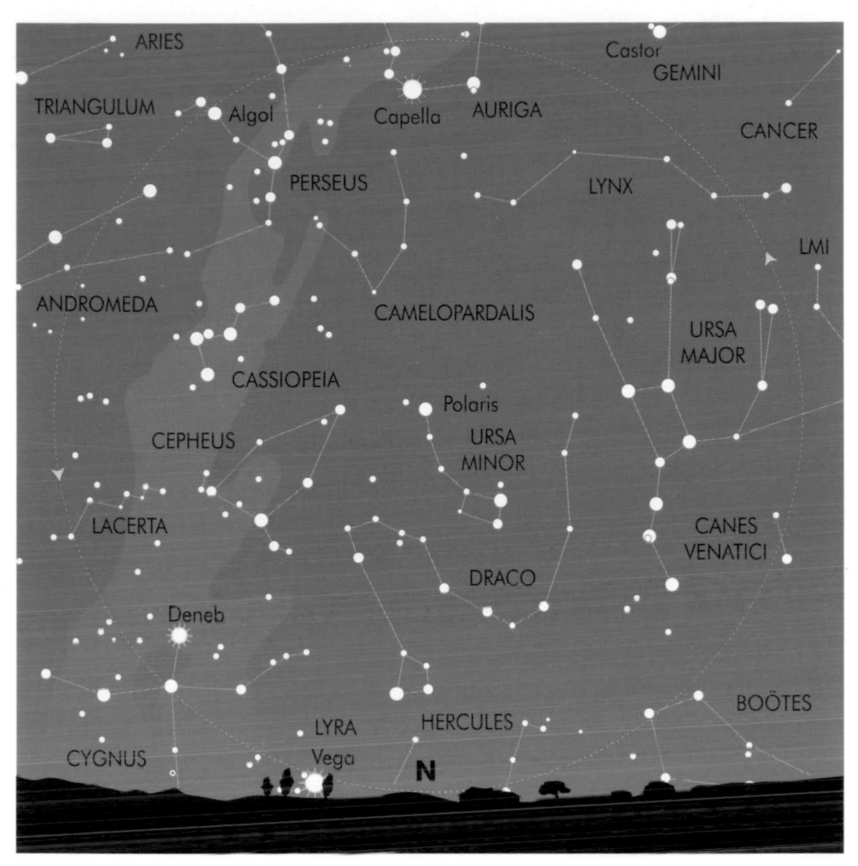

The circumpolar constellations for 50°N, which may be seen on any clear night

Right ascension is slightly more complicated. Although it corresponds to longitude on Earth, it is measured in hours, minutes, and seconds, like time, so 24 hours corresponds to 360°. It increases towards the east, so that as time passes, and the celestial sphere rotates towards the west, the right ascension on the meridian also increases. On Earth, however, longitude is measured east or west of a fixed meridian line, the one that passes through the centre of a specific telescope at the Old Royal Observatory at Greenwich. On the celestial sphere, the zero point for right ascension has been defined as the line that passes through the point where the Sun crosses the celestial equator from south to north, i.e., at the spring equinox. (This is the line with the numbered graduations.) The outermost scale shows right ascension, so although Star Finder's scale is small, it may be used to find the approximate position of any object in the sky. If the position of a new comet, for example, is given in right ascension and declination, you can use the graduations to see where and also when it will be visible.

THE POSITION OF THE MOON AND PLANETS

The movement of the Moon against the sky is extremely complex, so cannot be shown on a simple device like Star Finder. It ranges quite widely on either side of the ecliptic, so may be high in the sky at some times and low down towards the horizon at others. Luckily, it is generally easy to spot, because it is so bright, so a knowledge of its main phases will help you to judge when it is in the sky. The dates of New, First Quarter, Full, and Last Quarter are given in a diagram for each year. You can find its approximate position by using the meridian line on the overlay, in a method similar to the way in which you find the position of the Sun, and knowing that it moves eastwards against the stars.

At New, the Moon is usually above or below the Sun. (If it passes directly in front of the Sun, there is a solar eclipse somewhere in the world.) You can find the position of the Sun (and thus the Moon) at noon as described on p.6. At First Quarter, the Moon is 90° (6 hours) east of the Sun, so set 6 am against the date. The Moon will lie somewhere near the point where the meridian line crosses the ecliptic, usually higher or lower in the sky. At Full Moon, the Moon is opposite the Sun in the sky, so the approximate position is given if you set midnight against the date. And for Last Quarter, set 6 pm. For intermediate dates, you can roughly estimate the required difference in time (about 50 minutes per day).

The planets have complicated paths (the name comes from the Greek, *planetos*, meaning 'wandering'). Like the Moon they always lie within the Zodiac, which is shown in the diagrams opposite. Also like the Moon, the movements of the planets are generally from west to east, but they may also move in the opposite (or retrograde) direction, appearing to form loops or 'S-' or 'Z-shaped' paths in the sky. This is particularly noticeable for the planets outside the orbit of the Earth – of which Mars, Jupiter, and Saturn are visible to the naked eye – and a typical path is shown in the diagram. At such times these planets are near opposition – opposite the Sun in the sky, and are most clearly visible. The inner

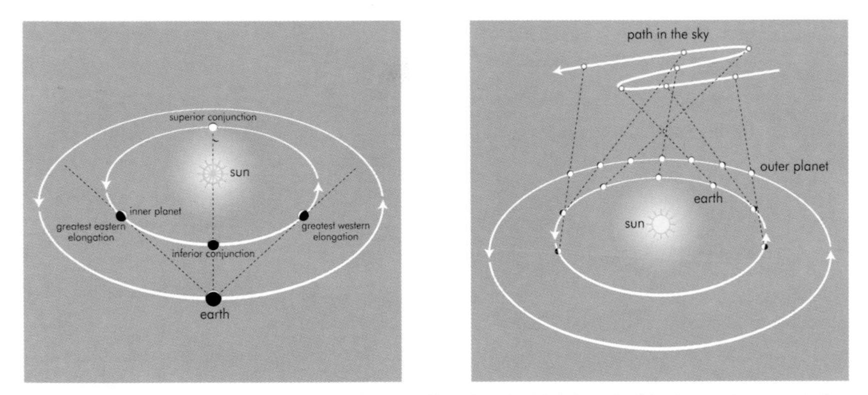

The retrograde movement of an outer planet against the sky (right), and of the inner planets relative to the Earth and Sun (left)

planets, Mercury and Venus, can never come to opposition, but are best seen when they are farthest from the Sun, at eastern or western elongation, which occur in the evening or early morning, respectively, and shown in the second diagram. Neither inner nor outer planets are visible around conjunction, when they appear close to the Sun in the sky.

This same term, conjunction, is used when any prominent celestial objects (such as the Moon and a planet, or two planets) are close together in the sky. Many such events occur, so only a few are mentioned here. Details are often given in newspapers and on TV and radio.

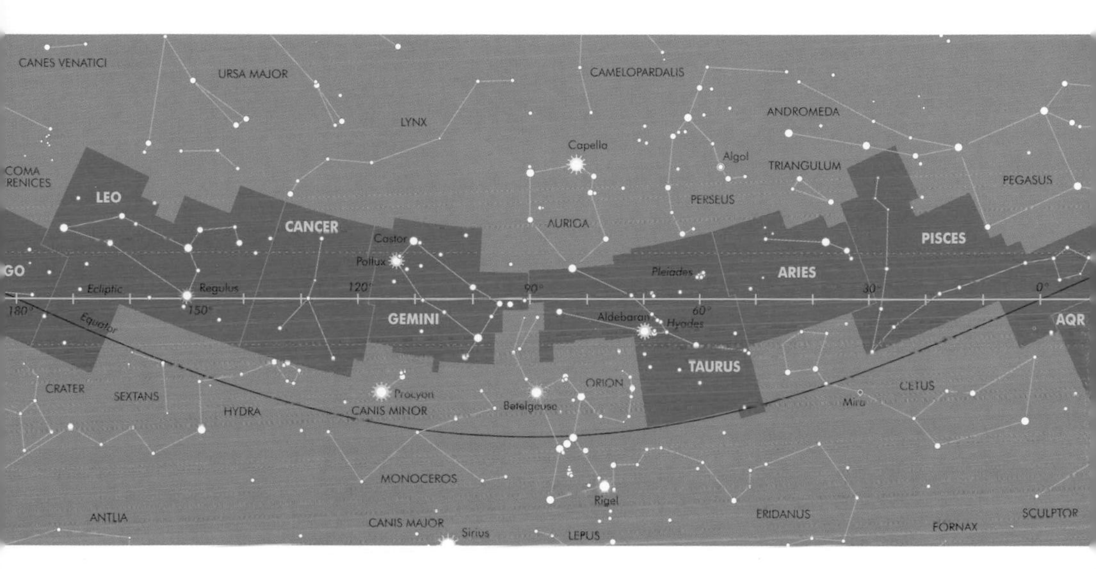

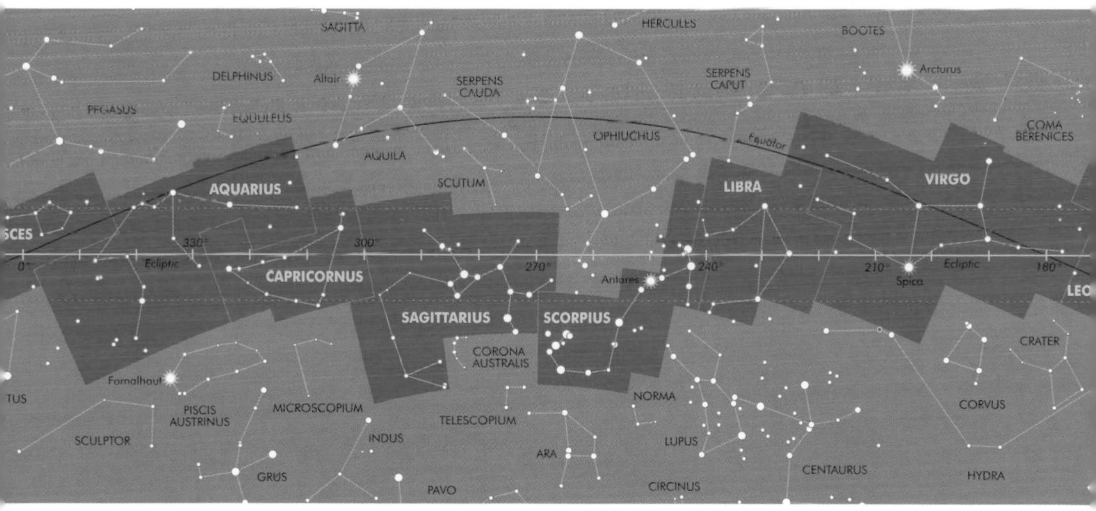

The constellations of the Zodiac are shown by the darker tint. The Moon and planets are always found within the zone marked by the dashed lines

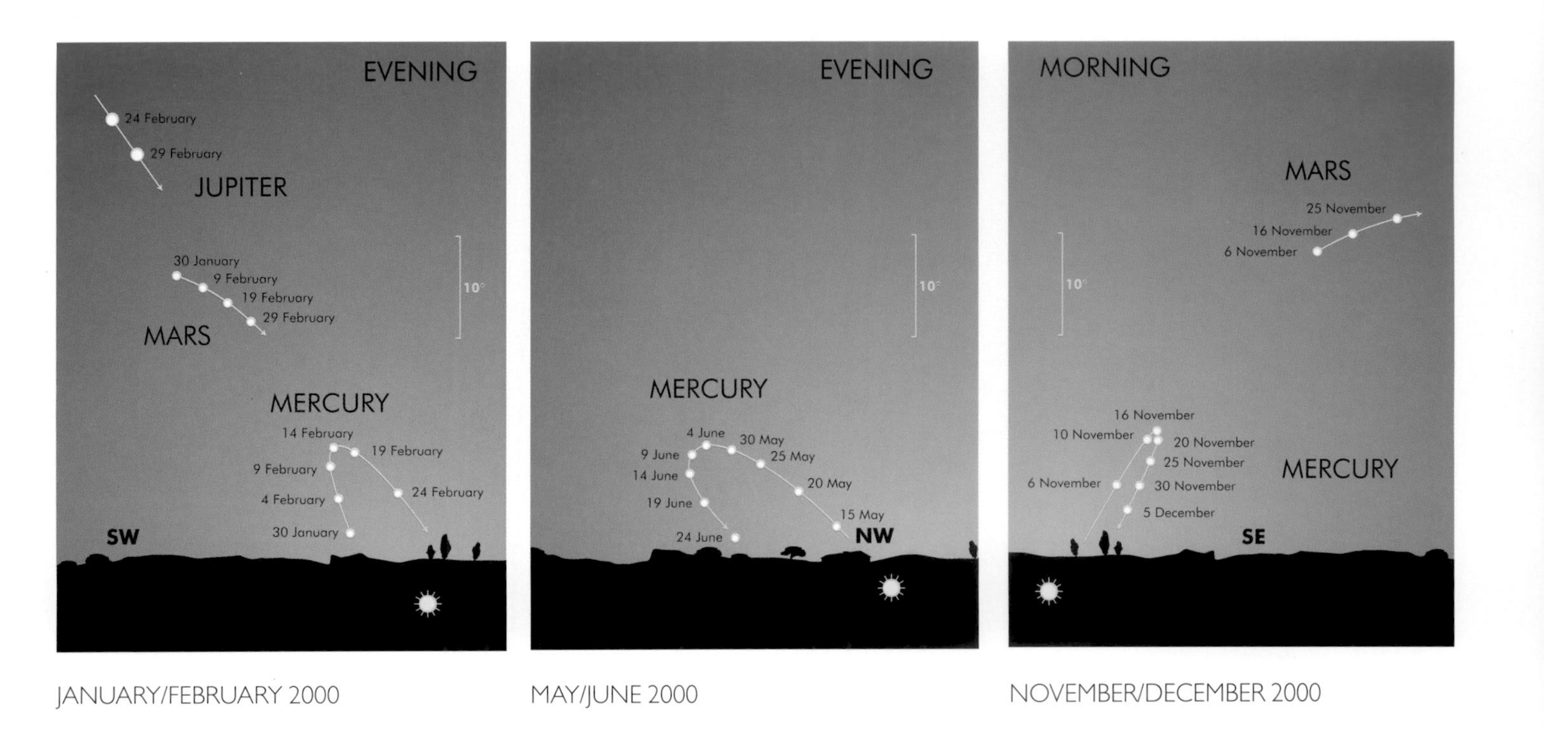

JANUARY/FEBRUARY 2000

MAY/JUNE 2000

NOVEMBER/DECEMBER 2000

PLANETARY POSITIONS 2000

Mercury is visible in the evening sky in the middle of February and mid-June, and also in the early morning in mid-November. Although brighter in January and May, it is then very close to the horizon.

Venus is not very easily visible this year, although it is very bright early in the year. It begins to appear in the evening twilight in late November and December.

SOLAR ECLIPSES 2000

Feb.05	Partial	Antarctica
July 01	Partial	SE Pacific, SW South America
July 31	Partial	NE Asia, Alaska, Canada, Greenland

LUNAR ECLIPSES 2000

Jan.21	Total	NW Asia, N & S America, Europe, N & W Africa
July 16	Total	Pacific, Antarctica, Australasia, SW Asia

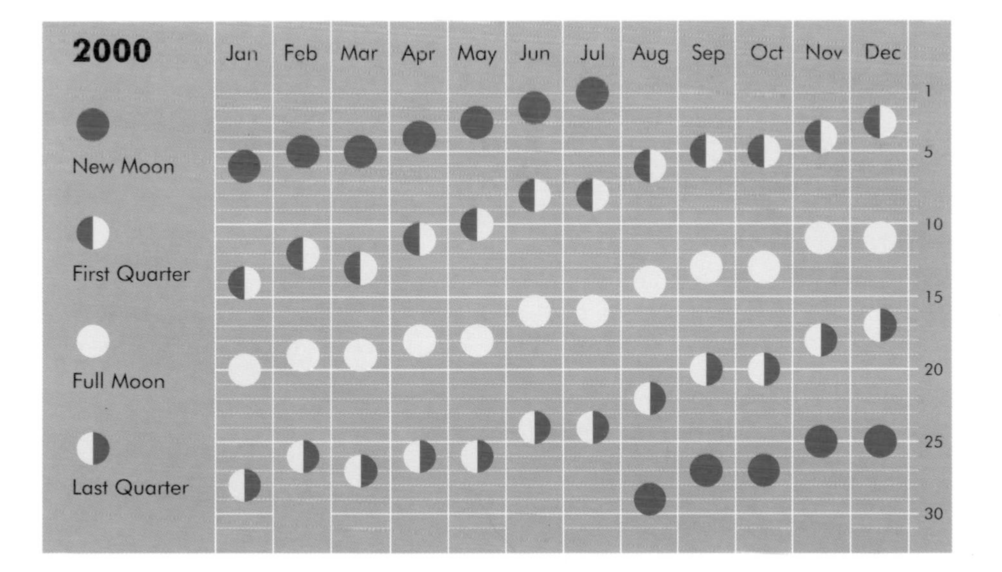

Mars 2000

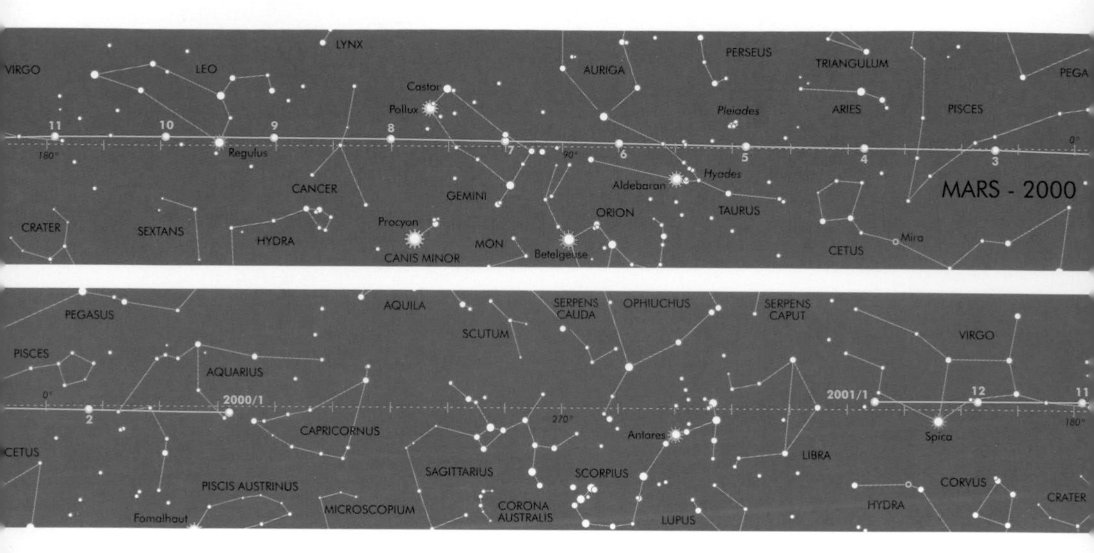

Mars does not come to opposition in 1999. It may be seen early in the year, in Aquarius and Pisces, until it disappears in twilight in April. There is a close conjunction with Jupiter on April 6 when both are in evening twilight. It reappears in the morning sky in September, in Leo, passing within 1° of Regulus on September 16. It becomes increasingly prominent towards the end of the year.

Jupiter and Saturn 2000

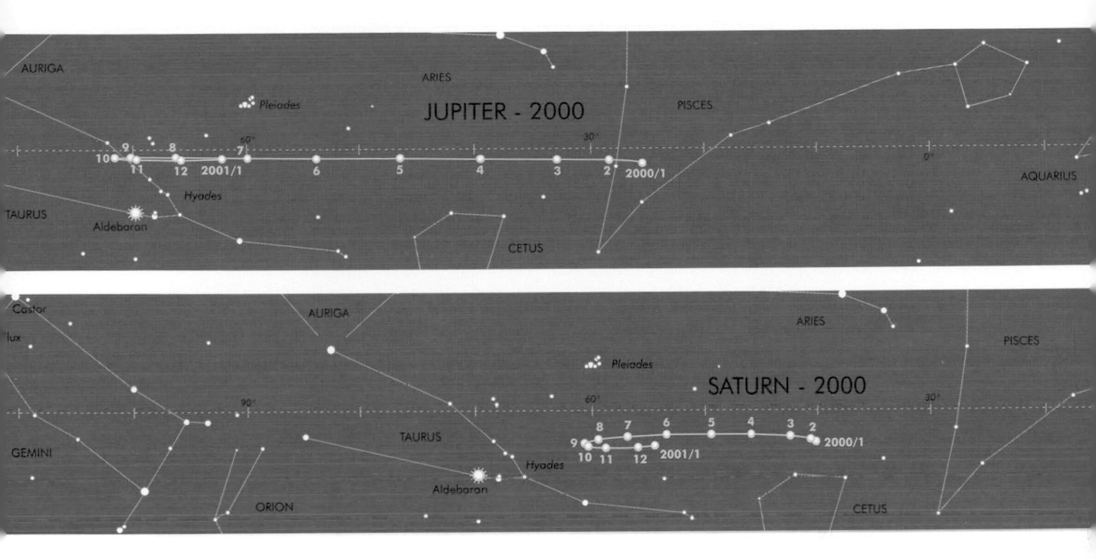

Jupiter, like Mars, is reasonably placed in the evening sky for the first couple of months, but it becomes too close to the Sun for observation in late April. It dominates the night sky later in the year, especially around opposition on November 28 (in Taurus), when it is very bright, reaching magnitude -2.9. It may then be seen throughout the night.

Saturn slowly moves from Aries into Taurus during the course of the year, and has a similar period of visibility to Jupiter, also coming too close to the Sun to be observed from late April. It is best seen in the latter half of the year. It is at opposition on November 19, at magnitude -0.9.

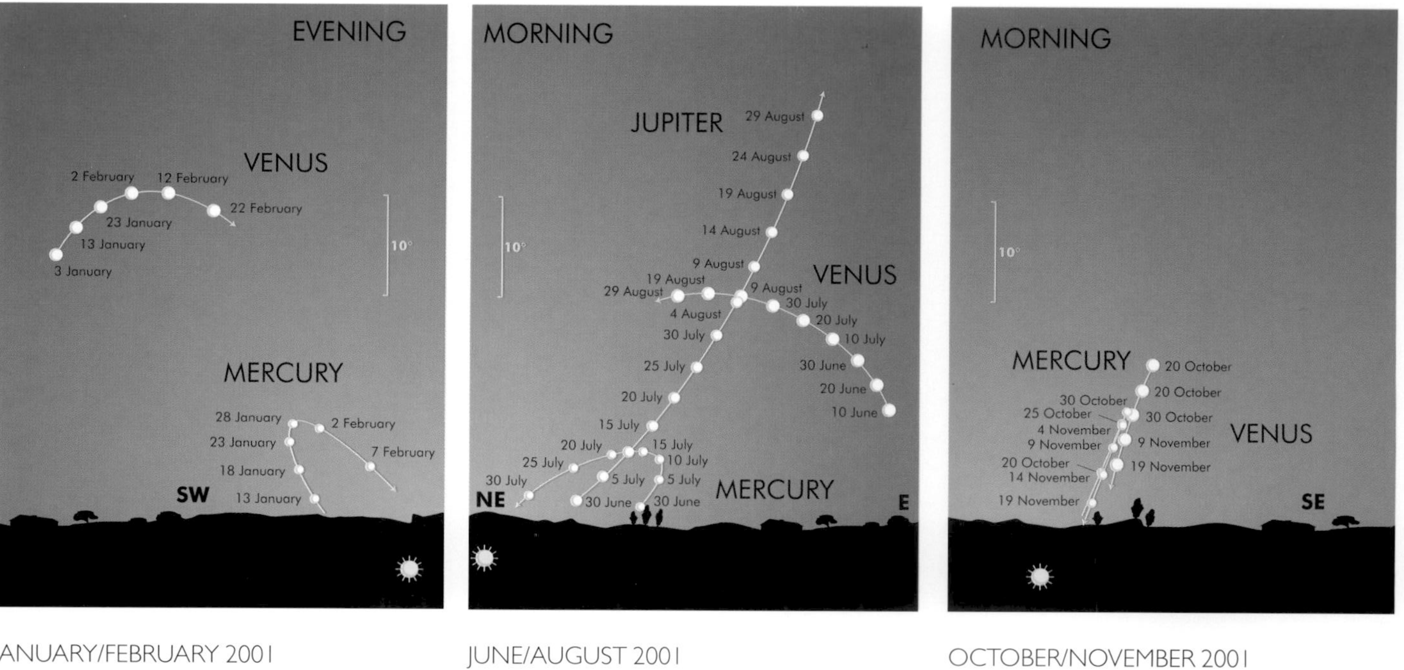

JANUARY/FEBRUARY 2001

JUNE/AUGUST 2001

OCTOBER/NOVEMBER 2001

PLANETARY POSITIONS 2001

Mercury is easiest to see in late January and late October, in the evening and morning skies, respectively. It may be glimpsed with difficulty in the morning in mid-July. On all three occasions, Venus is also in the same region of the sky. The two planets are within 1° of one another for 11 days in late October and early November.

Venus is prominent in the evening sky in January and February (when it reaches mag. -4.7), and again in October, when it will help to locate Mercury, although it is then closer to the horizon. It is reasonably easy to see in the middle of the year, when its magnitude is around -4.0.

SOLAR ECLIPSES 2001

Jun.21	Total	4m57s	South America, S & Central Africa
Dec.14	Annular	3m53s	Hawaii, SW Canada, W U.S.A., Mexico, Caribbean

LUNAR ECLIPSES 2001

Jan.09	Total	Australia, Indonesia, Philippines, Asia, Africa
Jly.05	Partial	Antarctica, Australia, New Zealand, parts of Asia

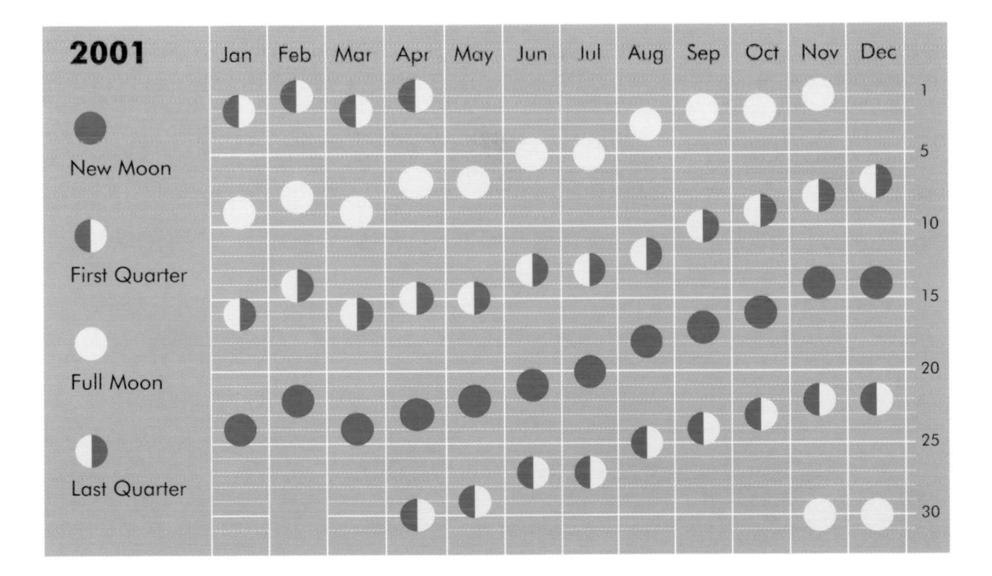

Mars 2001

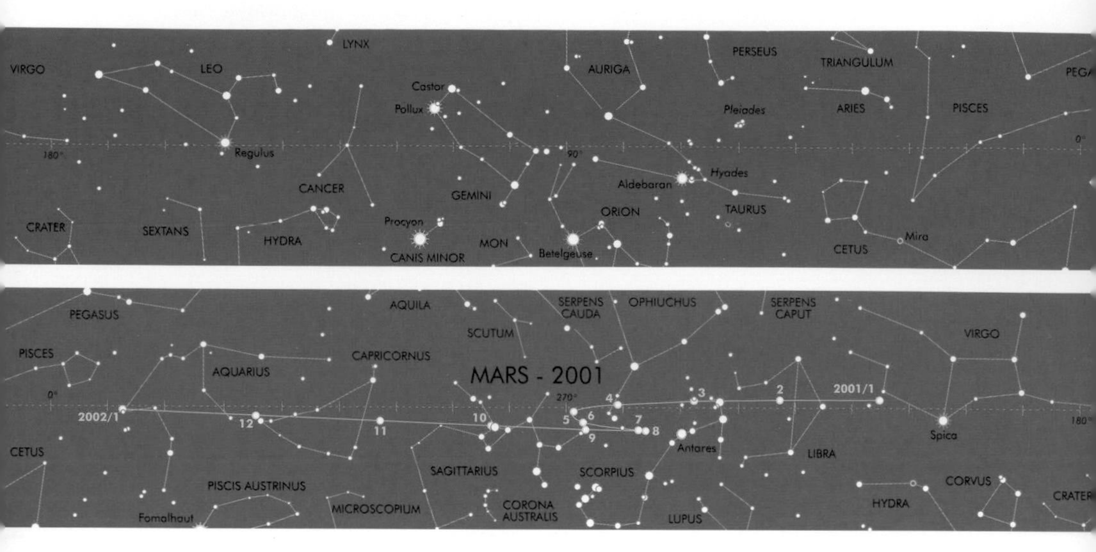

Mars is visible at some time of the night throughout most of the year. At opposition on June 14, it is on the borders of Ophiuchus and Sagittarius, almost at the lowest part of the ecliptic, but will then be in twilight. It is most readily seen early in the night late in the year. It is about 3°N of Spica in Virgo on November 20.

Jupiter and Saturn 2001

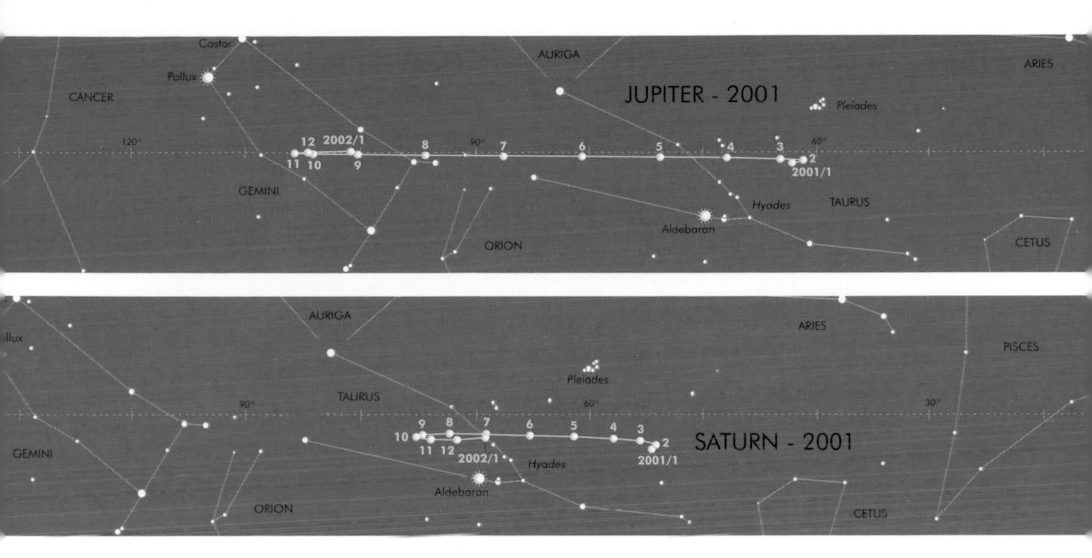

Jupiter does not come to opposition in 2001, but it is visible for a large part of the night until April. It reappears in the morning sky in late July, when it is close to Venus, and by December is visible throughout the night.

Saturn is also visible for a large part of the year. It is moderately bright in the early months (about -0.1 mag.) but reaches -0.4 at opposition on December 4, when it is in Taurus.

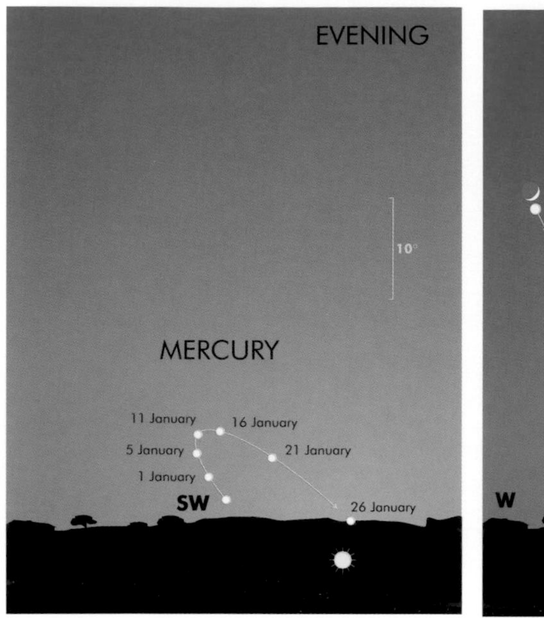

JANUARY 2002

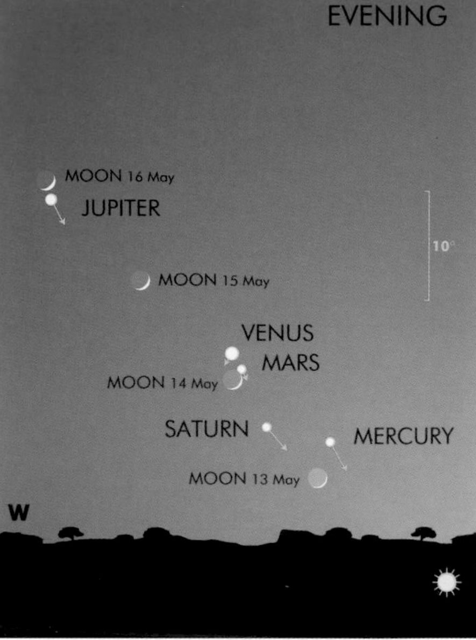

13–16 MAY 2002

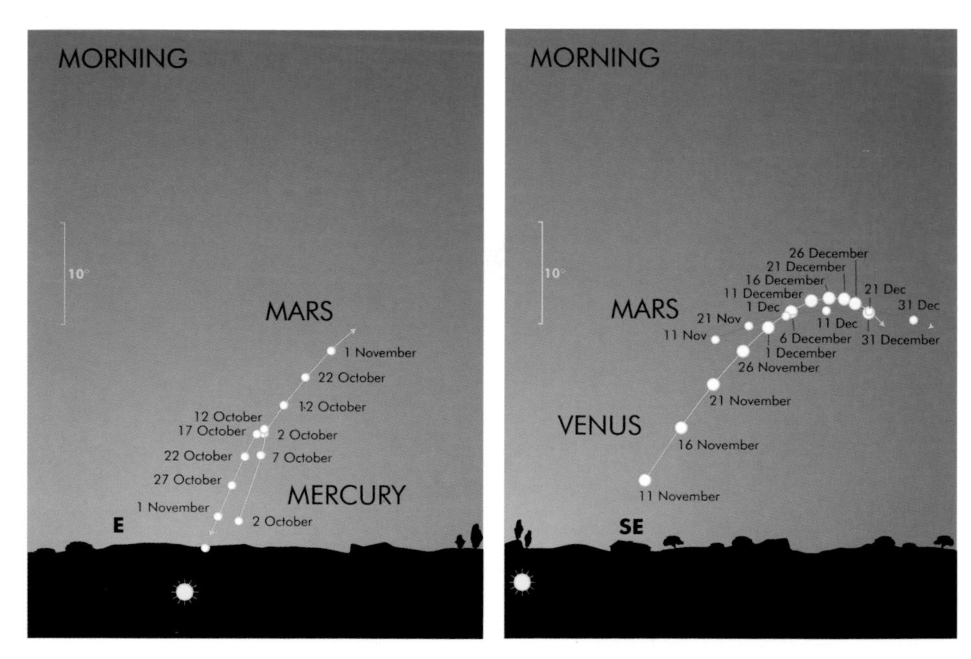

OCTOBER/NOVEMBER 2002

NOVEMBER/DECEMBER 2002

PLANETARY POSITIONS 2002

In a rare conjunction, all five planets Mercury, Venus, Mars, Jupiter and Saturn are visible in the western sky, accompanied by the crescent Moon, between May 13 and 16.

Mercury is visible in the west in January, but the morning apparition in mid-October is likely to be more favourable. It is appears close to Mars on October 10.

Venus is a brilliant morning object from early November until the end of the year. It reaches a magnitude of about -4.7 in early December. There is a conduction with Mars on December 6.

SOLAR ECLIPSES 2002

Jun.10–11	Annular	0m23s	SE Asia, Philippines, North America (not N and E)
Dec.04	Total	2m04s	S. Africa, Madagascar, S & W Australia

LUNAR ECLIPSES 2002

There are no total or partial lunar eclipses in 2002

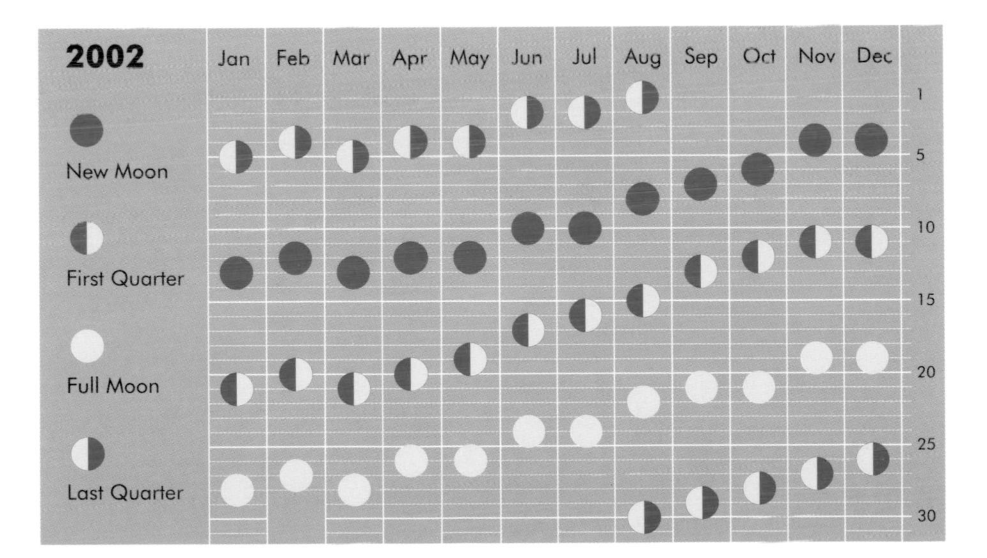

Mars 2002

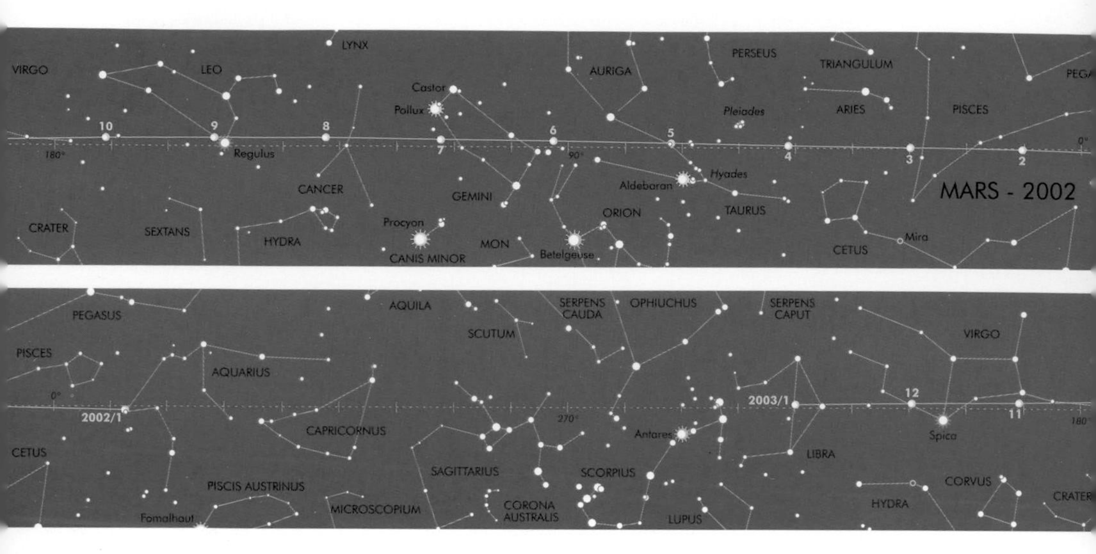

Mars is an evening object in the first quarter of the year and forms a small triangle with Venus and Saturn on May 7. It is invisible from the end of May until October. It is within 2° of Venus on December 12, but does not have an opposition in 2000, so never becomes particularly bright.

Jupiter and Saturn 2002

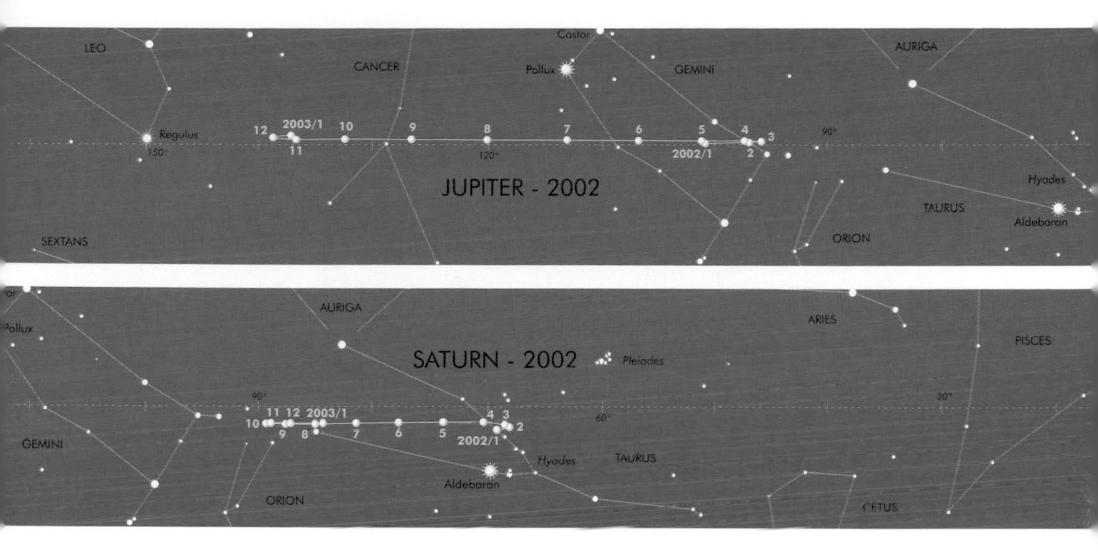

Jupiter is at opposition on January 1 at about mag. -2.6, but slowly declines to about -2.0 before it disappears into twilight in late May. It reappears after midnight in August, brightening and becoming visible longer each night until the end of the year.

Saturn is in Taurus, to the west of Jupiter, and both disappears (in early May) and reappears (in July) slightly earlier than the larger planet. On May 7, it is close to both Venus and Mars in the sky. From a minimum of about mag. +0.1 it brightens to about -0.5 at opposition on December 18.

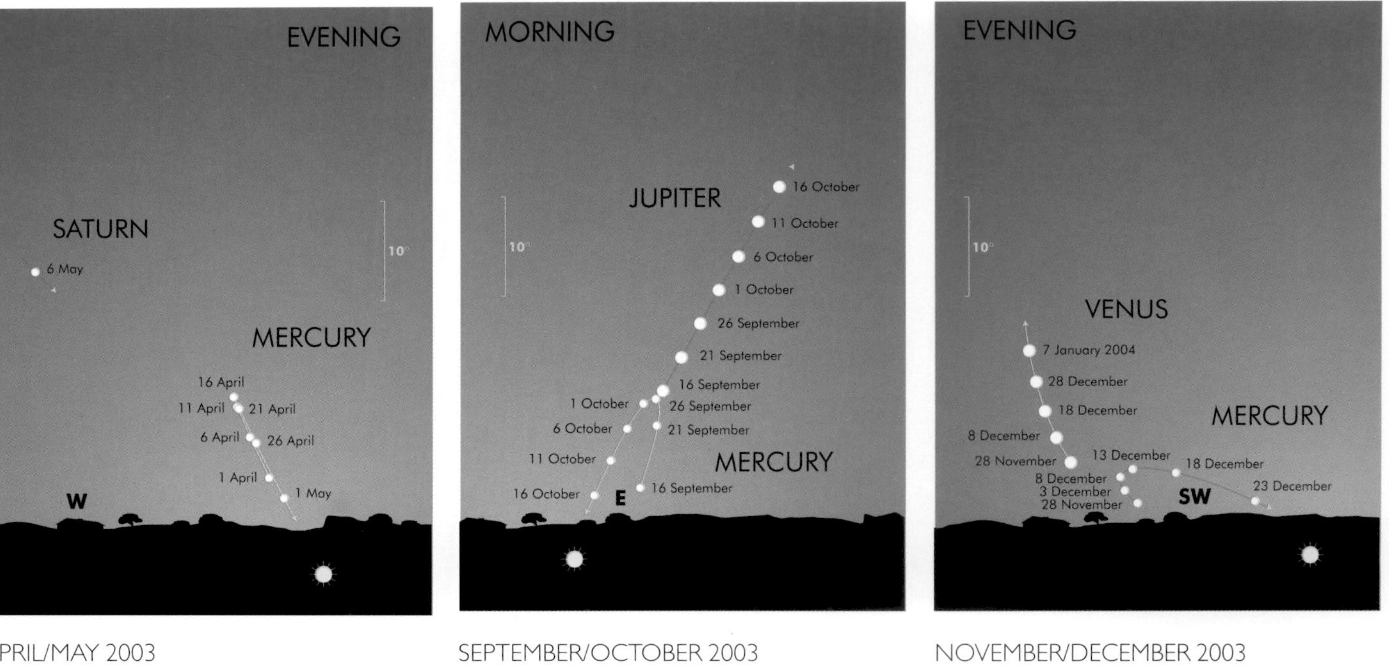

APRIL/MAY 2003

SEPTEMBER/OCTOBER 2003

NOVEMBER/DECEMBER 2003

PLANETARY POSITIONS 2003

Mercury has three apparitions, those for mid-April and September/October being the most favourable, while that for December is rather low on the horizon. On May 7, Mercury passes between the Sun and the Earth, when it takes about 5 hours 18 minutes to transit the Sun's disk. Viewing such a transit requires all the precautions used for observing the Sun. The safest method is to project the image on a white card, as described in *Wild Guide Night Sky* (p.129). There will be another transit in 2006.

Venus is best seen either as a morning object early in the year, or on December evenings, when it is brightening rapidly, and getting farther above the horizon.

SOLAR ECLIPSES 2003

May.31	Annular	3m37s	Arctic regions, Greenland, Iceland, N Europe, N Asia, Alaska, N Canada
Nov.23–24	Total	1m57s	Antarctica, S Australasia, S South America

LUNAR ECLIPSES 2003

May.16	Total	Antarctica, Africa, Europe, S & most of N America
Nov.08–9	Total	W Asia, Europe, N America

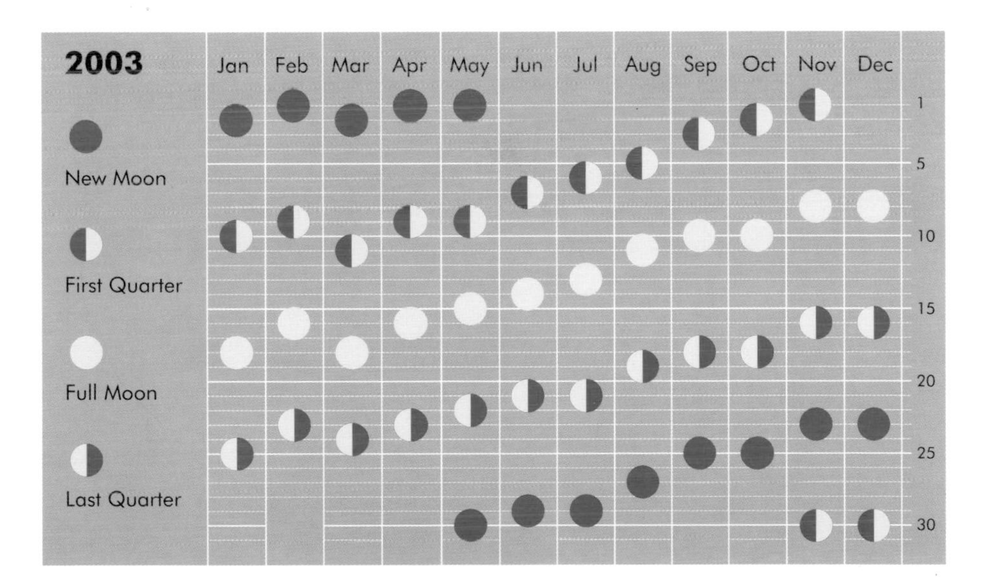

Mars 2003

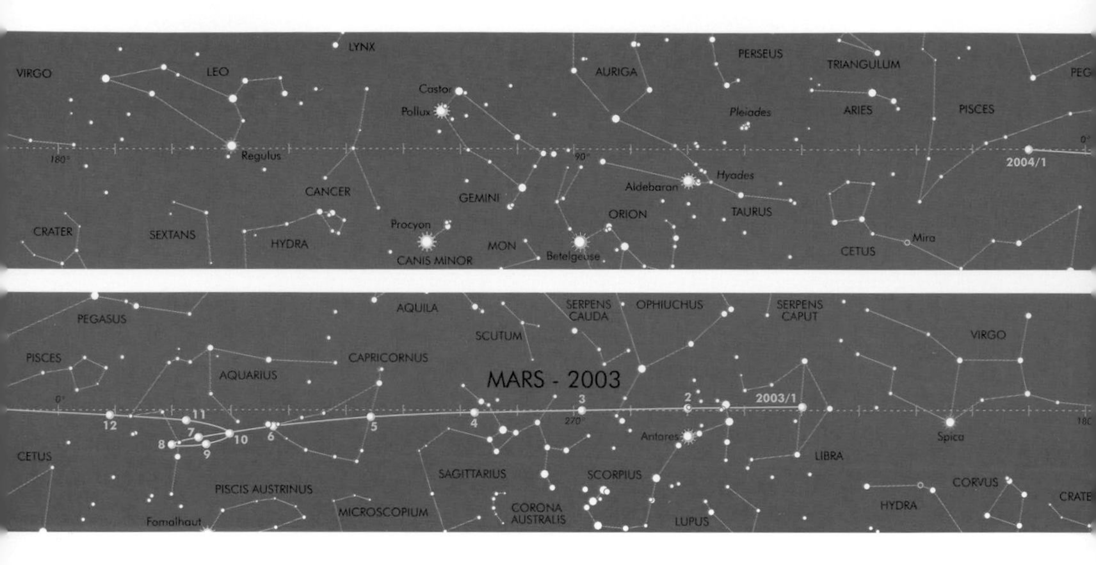

Mars may be seen for several months early in the year, but tends to be close to the horizon. Visibility rapidly improves from early July, and opposition is on August 29, at mag. -2.9.

Jupiter and Saturn 2003

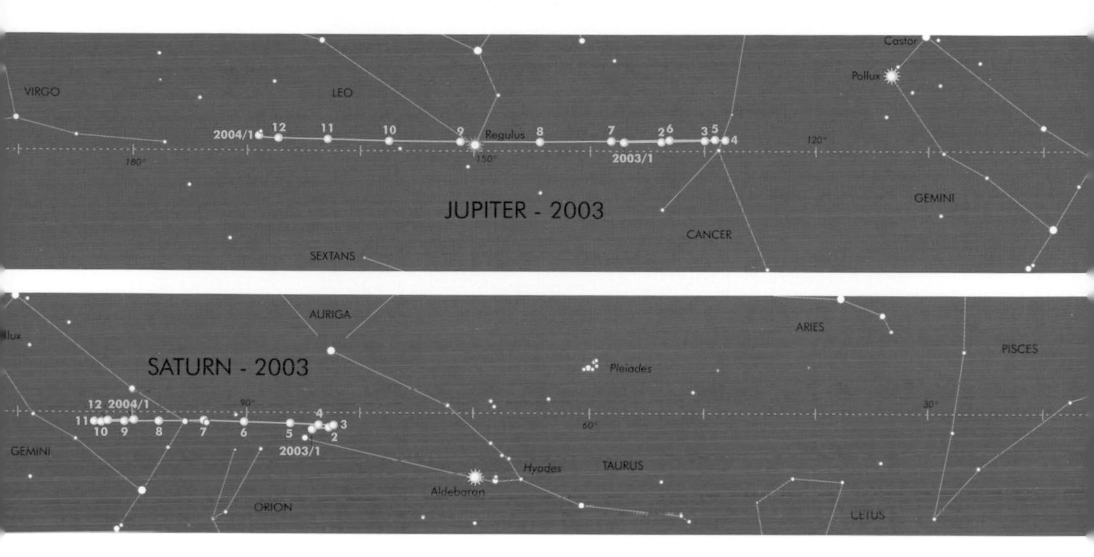

Jupiter has an extended period of visibility early in the year, with opposition in Cancer on February 2, at mag. -2.6. It reappears in the morning sky in September, and rises around midnight at the end of the year.

Saturn is visible for most of the night early in the year, but slowly fades, and is lost in twilight by May. It reappears in the early morning in July and by early December is visible throughout the night once more. Opposition occurs at 23:00 on December 31.

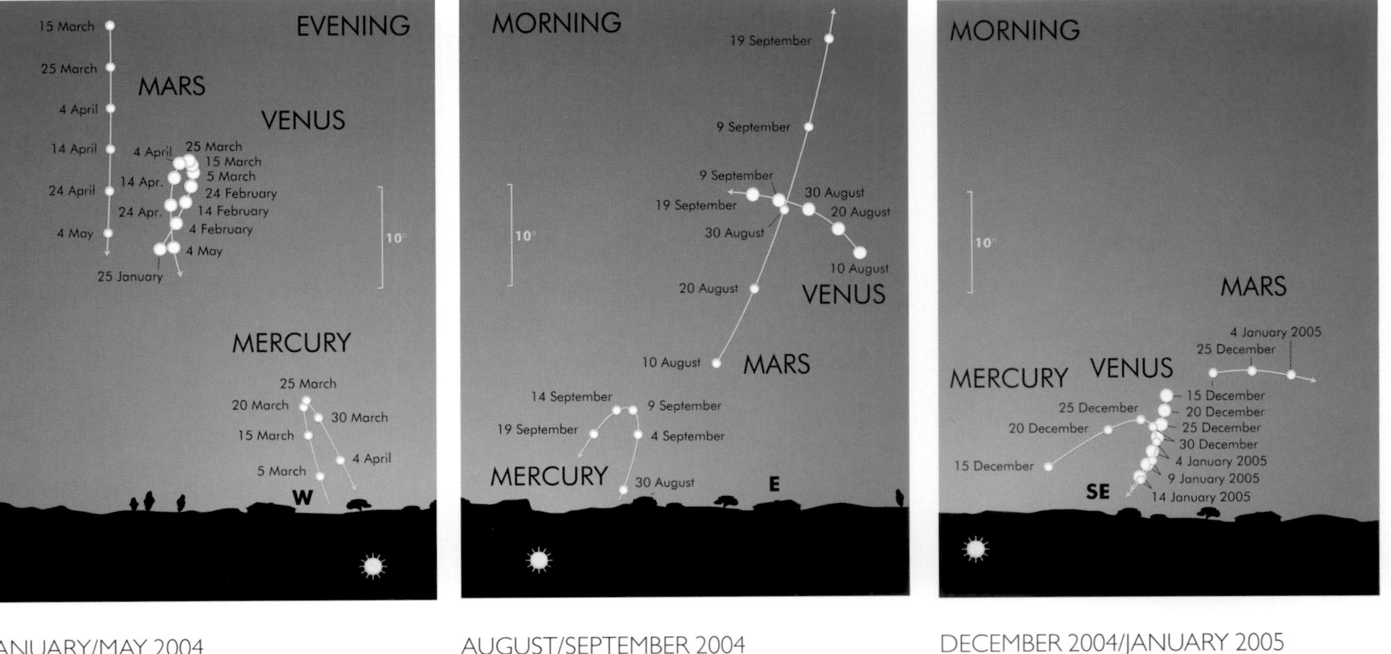

JANUARY/MAY 2004

AUGUST/SEPTEMBER 2004

DECEMBER 2004/JANUARY 2005

PLANETARY POSITIONS 2004

Mercury is at eastern elongation on March 30, and at western on September 10, when it is close to Regulus. It is probably easiest to see at western elongation in December, when there is a series of 5 close conjunctions with Venus, the first on December 28.

Venus is particularly conspicuous around its greatest eastern elongation on March 29, and western on August 17. On both occasions, Mars is close by in the sky. On June 4, there is one of the rare transits of Venus when it passes directly between the Sun and the Earth. (The last transit was in 1882 and the next is in 2012.) Experienced observers, who know how to take the proper precautions to observe the Sun safely, such as by projection, will be able to see Venus as a dark spot that takes about 6 hours 12 minutes to cross the Sun's disk. Late in the year, in December, Venus is close to Mercury, and should help with finding the latter planet in the twilight.

SOLAR ECLIPSES 2004

Apr.19	Partial	S Africa, Madagascar, Antarctica
Oct.14	Partial	Siberia, N China, Japan

LUNAR ECLIPSES 2004

May.04	Total	India, Middle East, Africa, Europe
Oct.28	Total	Europe, N & S America

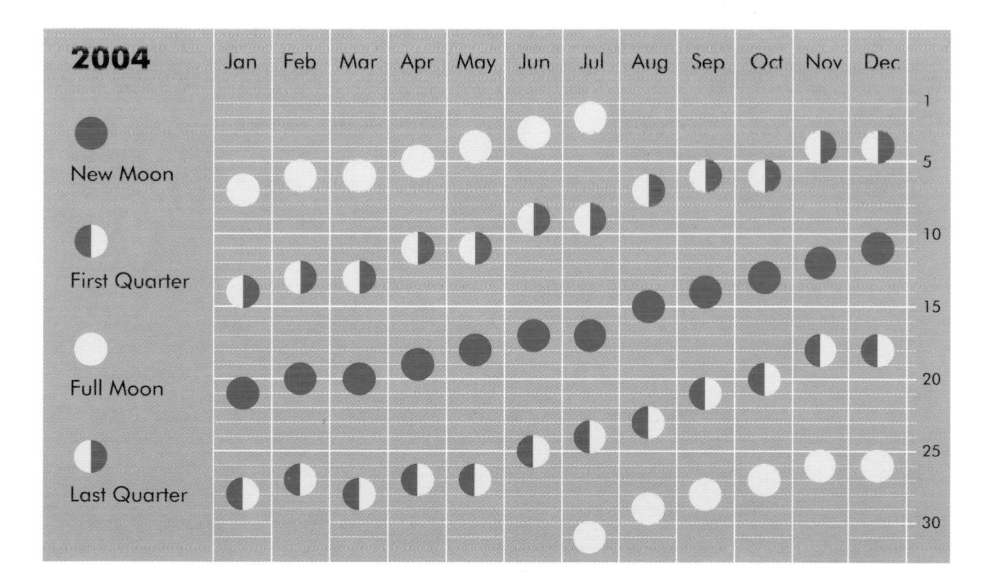

Mars 2004

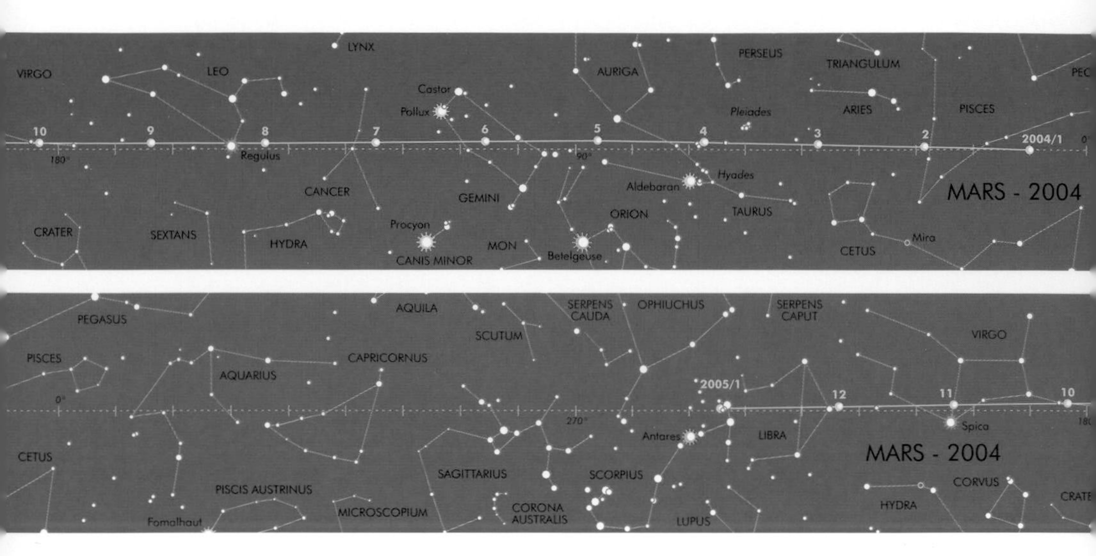

Mars is visible in the early part of 2004, disappearing into evening twilight in May, when it is in Taurus. It does not reach opposition in 2004, but reappears in the dawn sky in November.

Jupiter and Saturn 2004

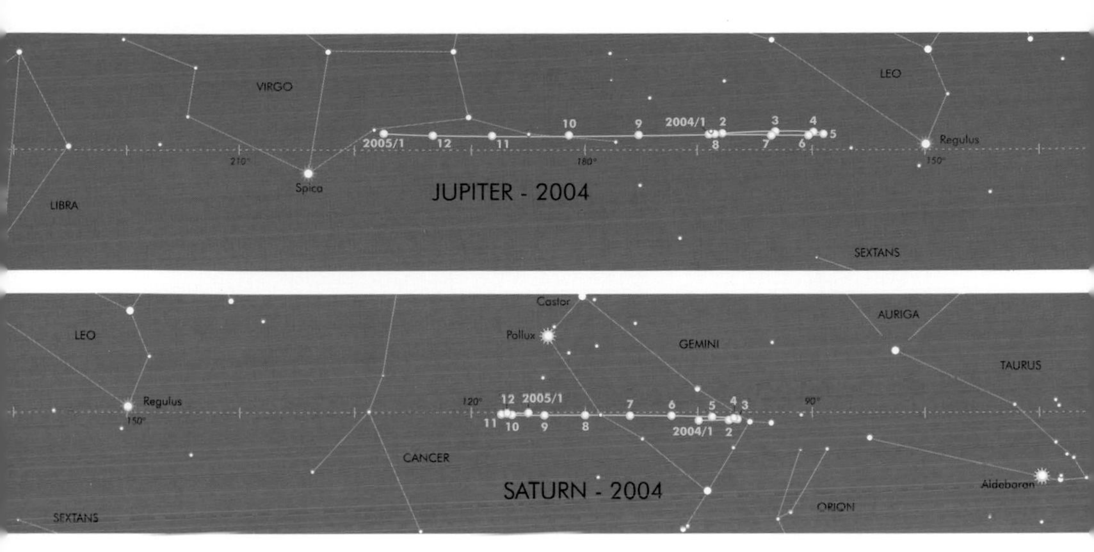

Jupiter is very bright in the morning sky early in the year, rising to -2.5 mag at opposition on March 4. It enters evening twilight in late May. It reappears at about -2.0 mag in the dawn twilight at the beginning of November.

Saturn has no opposition in 2004, but is visible for much of the year in Gemini. It fades from -0.5 mag in January to around 0.2 mag in mid-May, when it enters evening twilight. It reappears at dawn, slightly fainter, in September, close to the border of Cancer, then begins its retrograde motion in November before coming to opposition on 2005 January 14.

WHAT NEXT?

The following books, magazines, CD-ROMs, and societies provide more information on astronomy and the night sky:

Books

Dunlop, S. & Tirion, W., 1999, *Wild Guide Night Sky*, HarperCollins*Publishers*

Illingworth, V. (ed.), 1994, *Collins Dictionary of Astronomy*, HarperCollins*Publishers*

Karkoschka, E., 1990, *The Observer's Sky Atlas*, Springer-Verlag

Maris Multimedia, 1998, *Redshift 3*, CD-ROM, Dorling-Kindersley

Moore, P. (ed.), 1995, *The Observational Amateur Astronomer*, Springer-Verlag

Ridpath, I. & Tirion, W., 1993, *Collins Pocket Guide Stars & Planets*, 2nd edn., HarperCollins*Publishers* (3rd edn to be published January 2001)

Ridpath, I. (ed.), 1998, *Norton's Star Atlas*, 19th edn., Longman

Rükl, A., 1990, *Atlas of the Moon*, Hamlyn

Tirion, W., 1996, *Cambridge Star Atlas*, Cambridge University Press

Tirion, W. & Sinnott, R., 1998, *Sky Atlas 2000.0*, 2nd edn, Cambridge University Press

Magazines

Astronomy, Astro Media Corp., Milwaukee

Astronomy Now, Intra Press, London

Sky & Telescope, Sky Publishing Corp., Cambridge, Mass.

Societies

British Astronomical Association, Burlington House, Piccadilly, London W1V 9AG

The leading organisation for amateurs, founded in 1890, with a particular emphasis on observational work. It publishes a bi-monthly journal, which is recognized by amateur and professional astronomers worldwide for both popular articles and for the publication of accurate scientific research.

Royal Astronomical Society of Canada, 136 Dupont Street, Toronto, Ontario M5R 1V2

An organisation for both amateur and professional astronomers, with various regional centres across Canada. Its publications include an excellent yearly handbook, as well as a quarterly journal.

Society for Popular Astronomy, 36 Fairway, Keyworth, Nottingham NG12 5DU

An organisation intended for beginning amateur astronomers of all ages, particularly those without a great deal of equipment. It encourages amateurs to carry out simple observational programmes. Publishes a quarterly journal, *Popular Astronomy*, with readable, non-technical articles.